Endpaper Adult Coloring Book

Volume 1 in the Bibliophile Adult Coloring Books Series

Bibliophile Mania

ISBN-13: 978-1516934300
ISBN-10: 151693430X

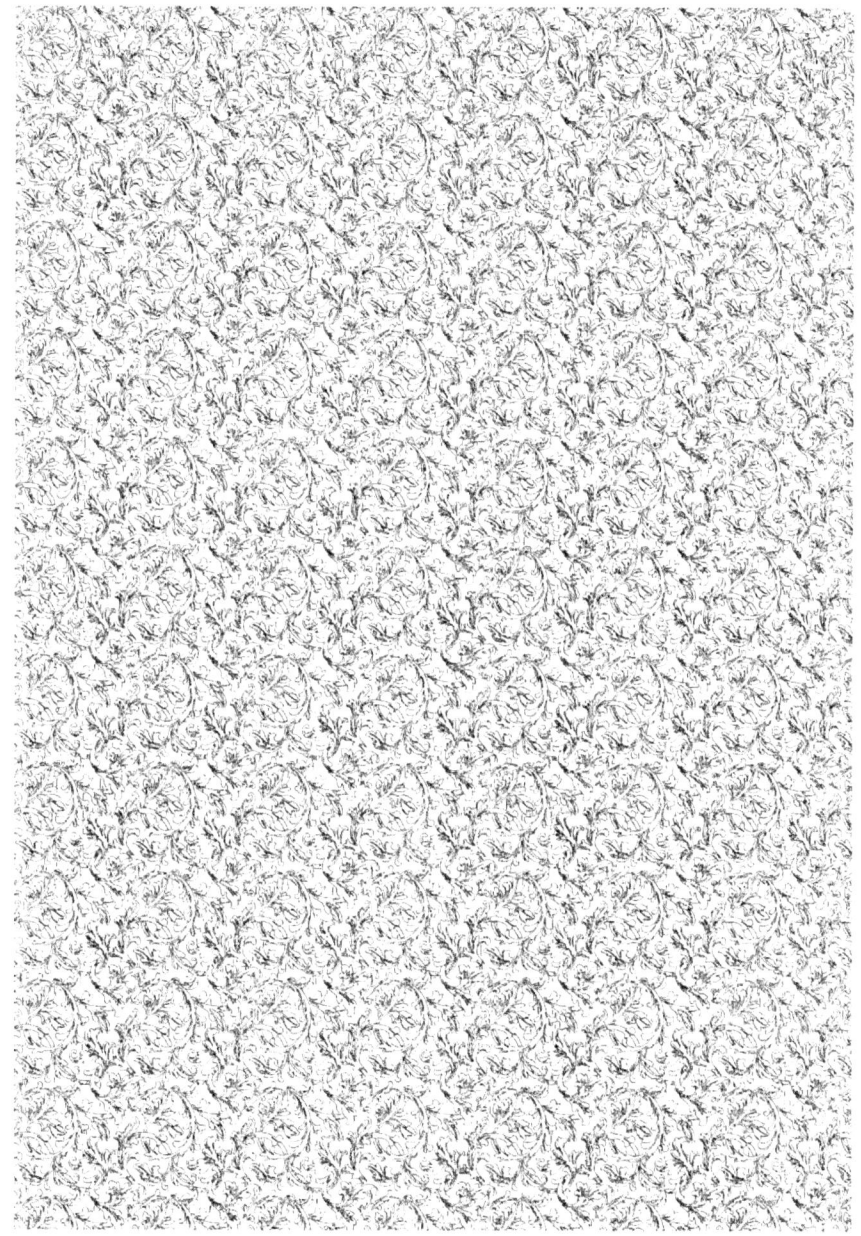

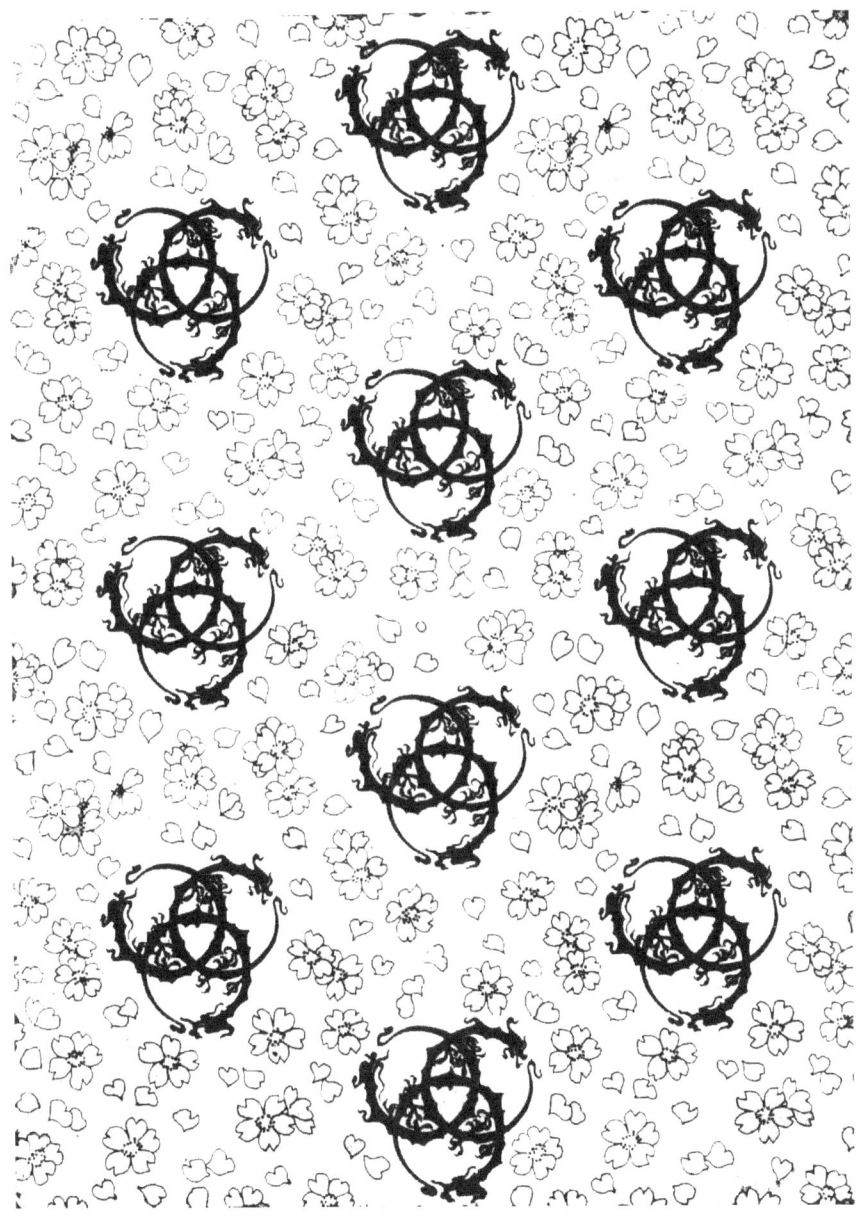

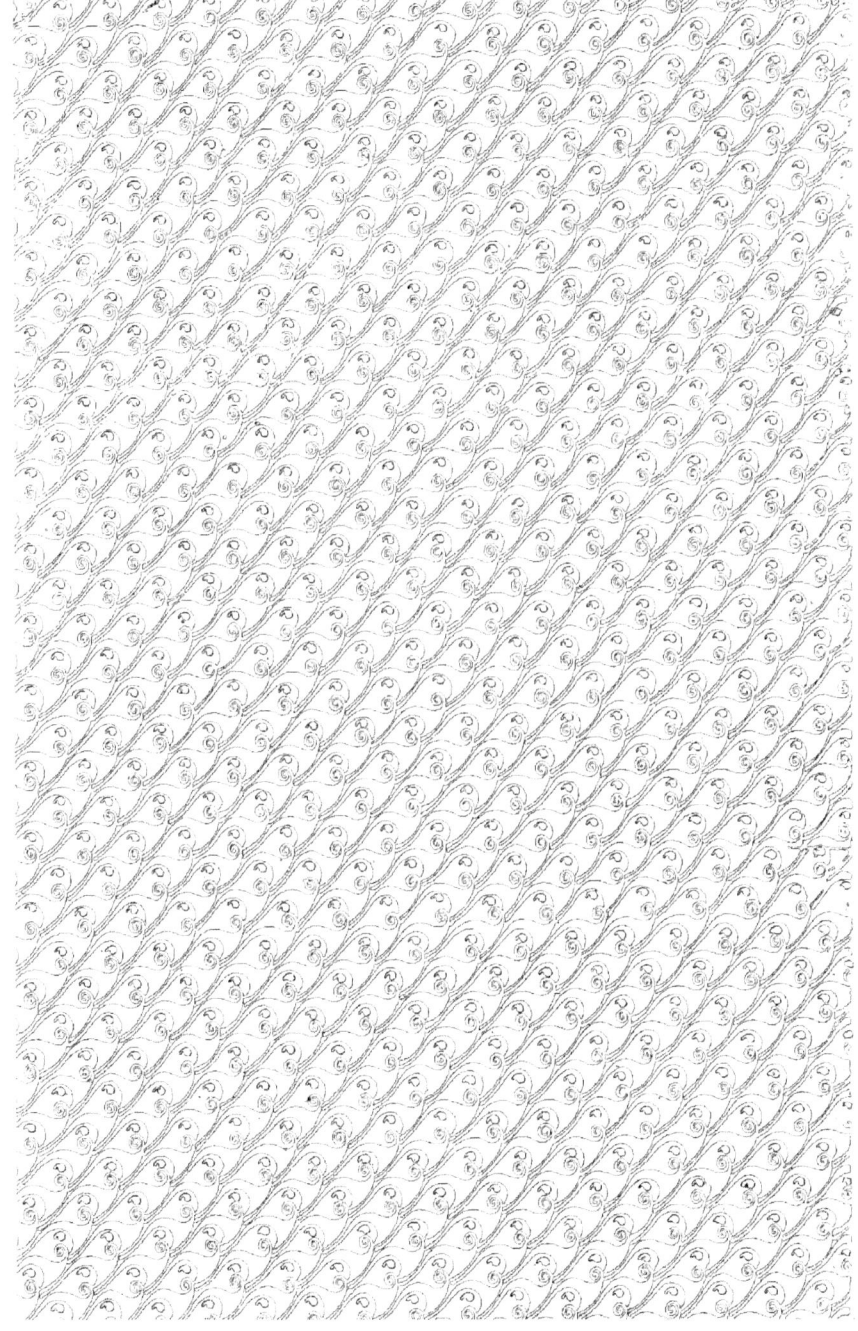

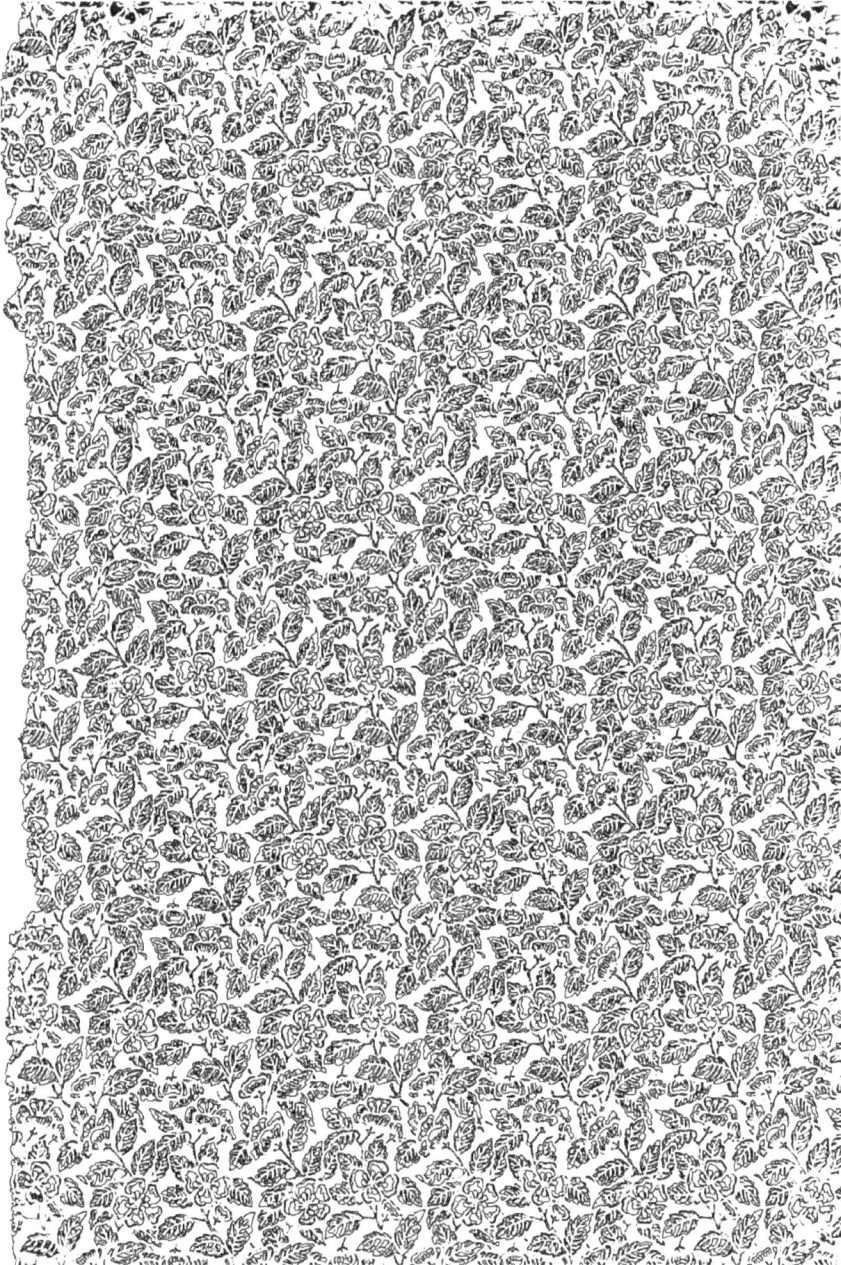

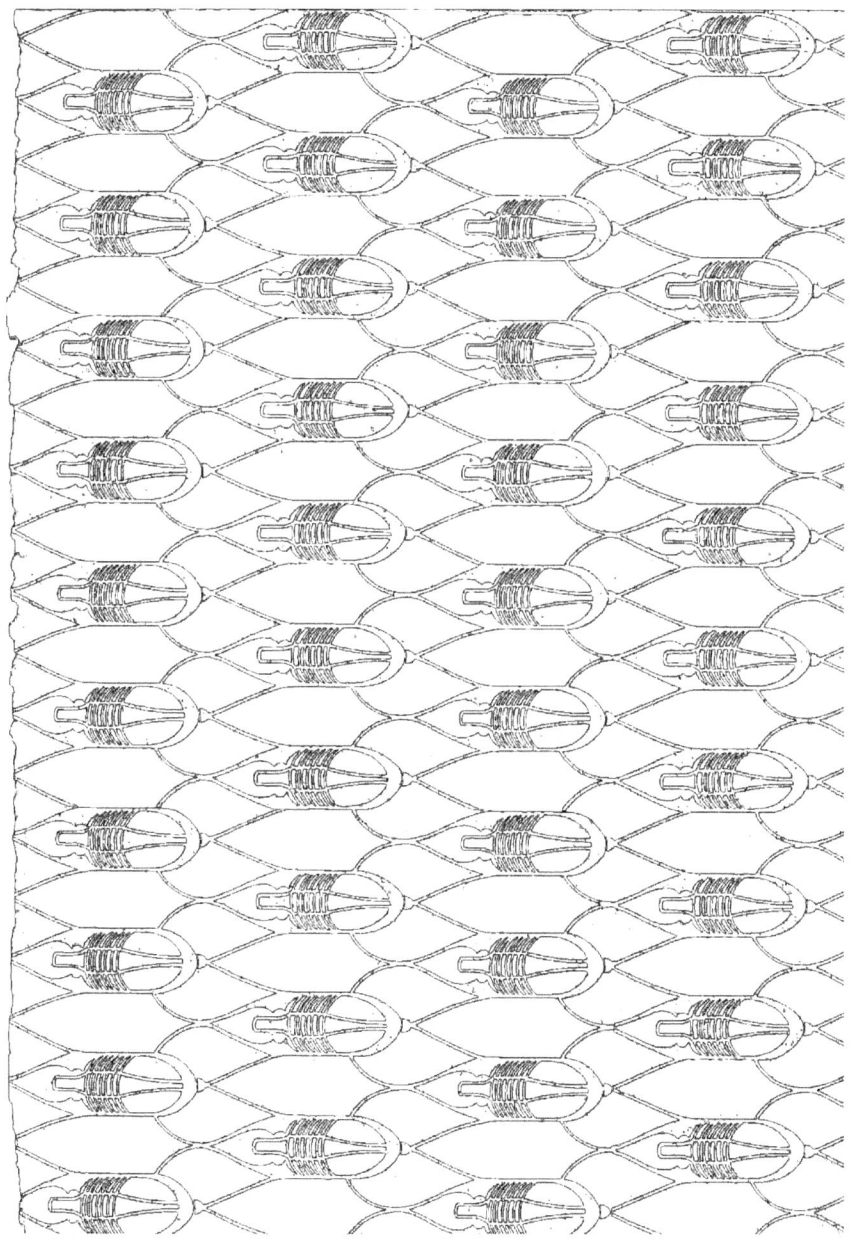

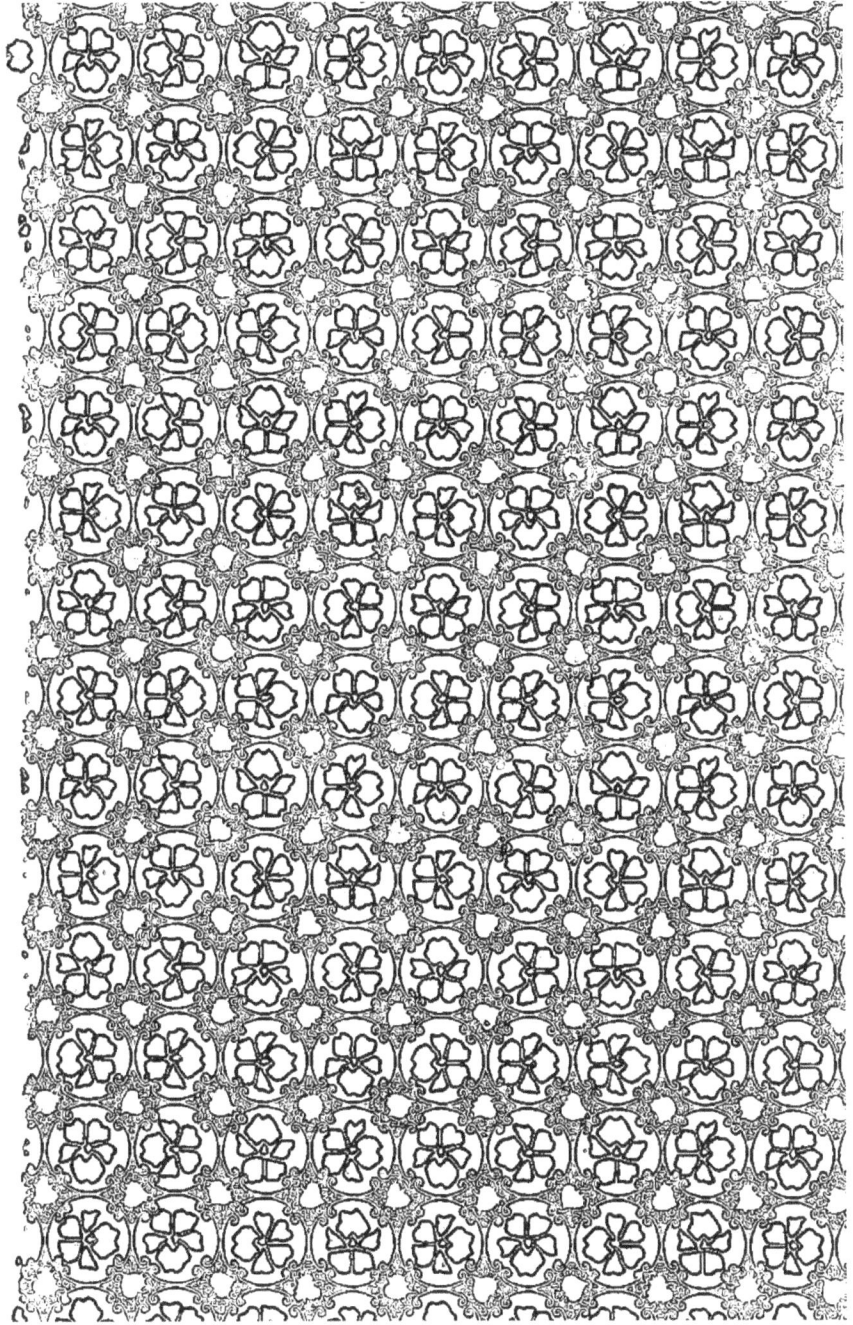

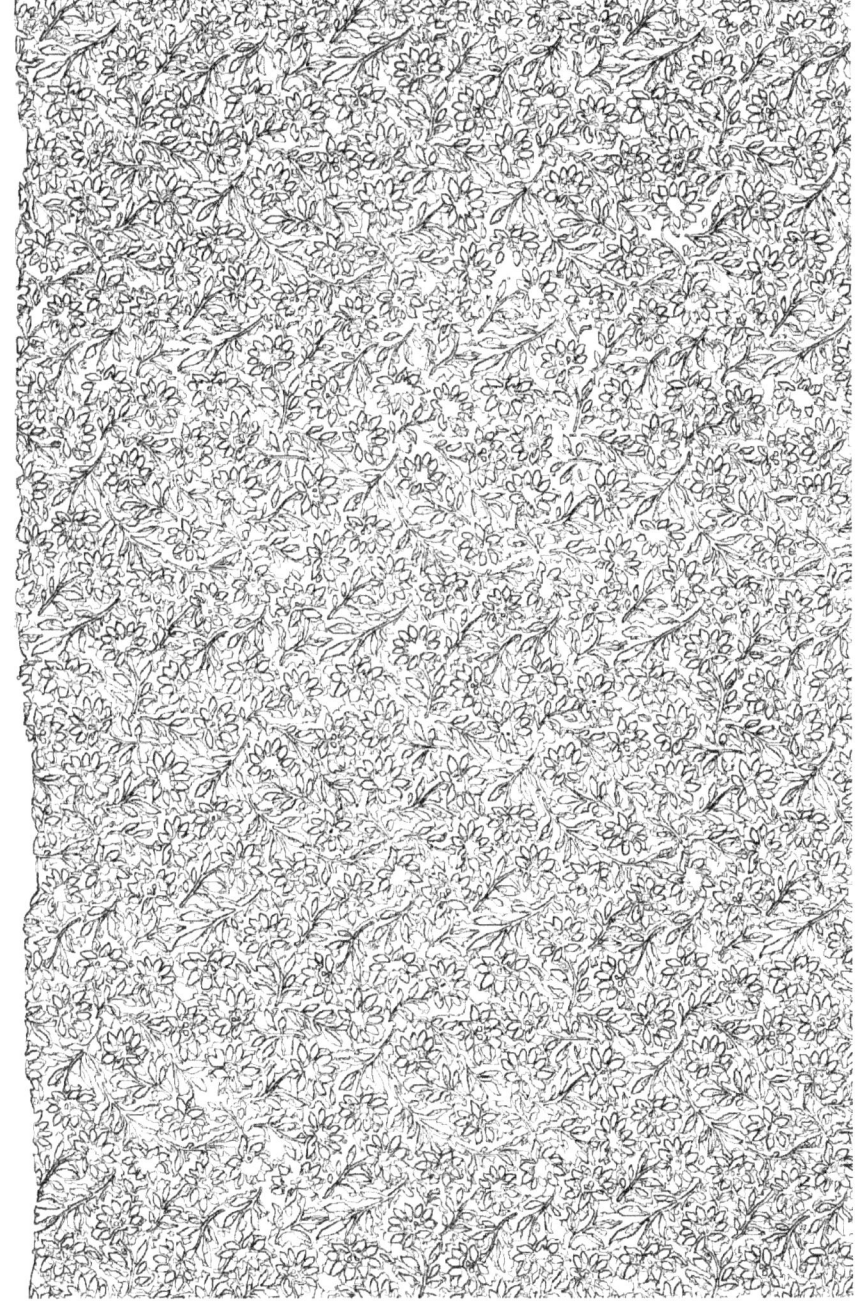

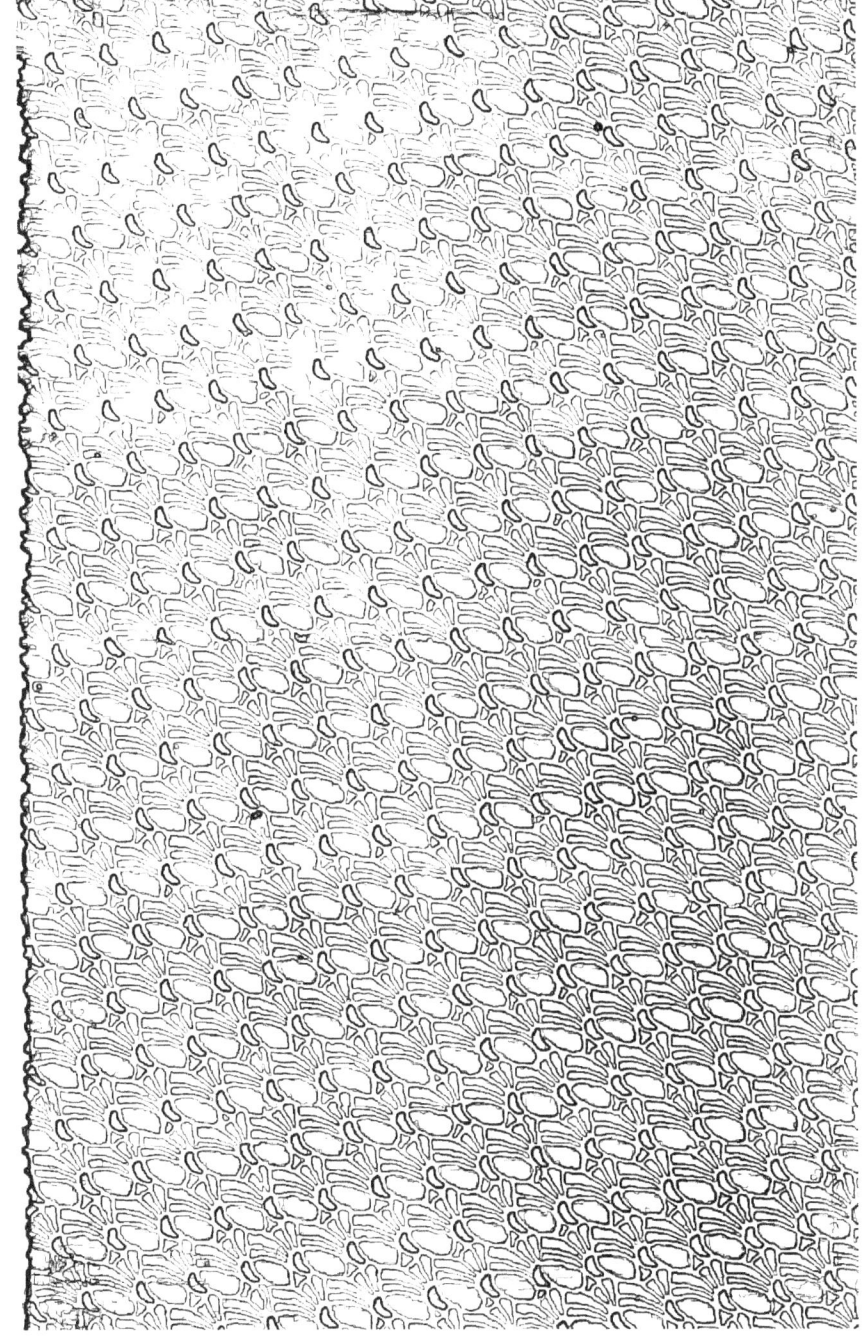

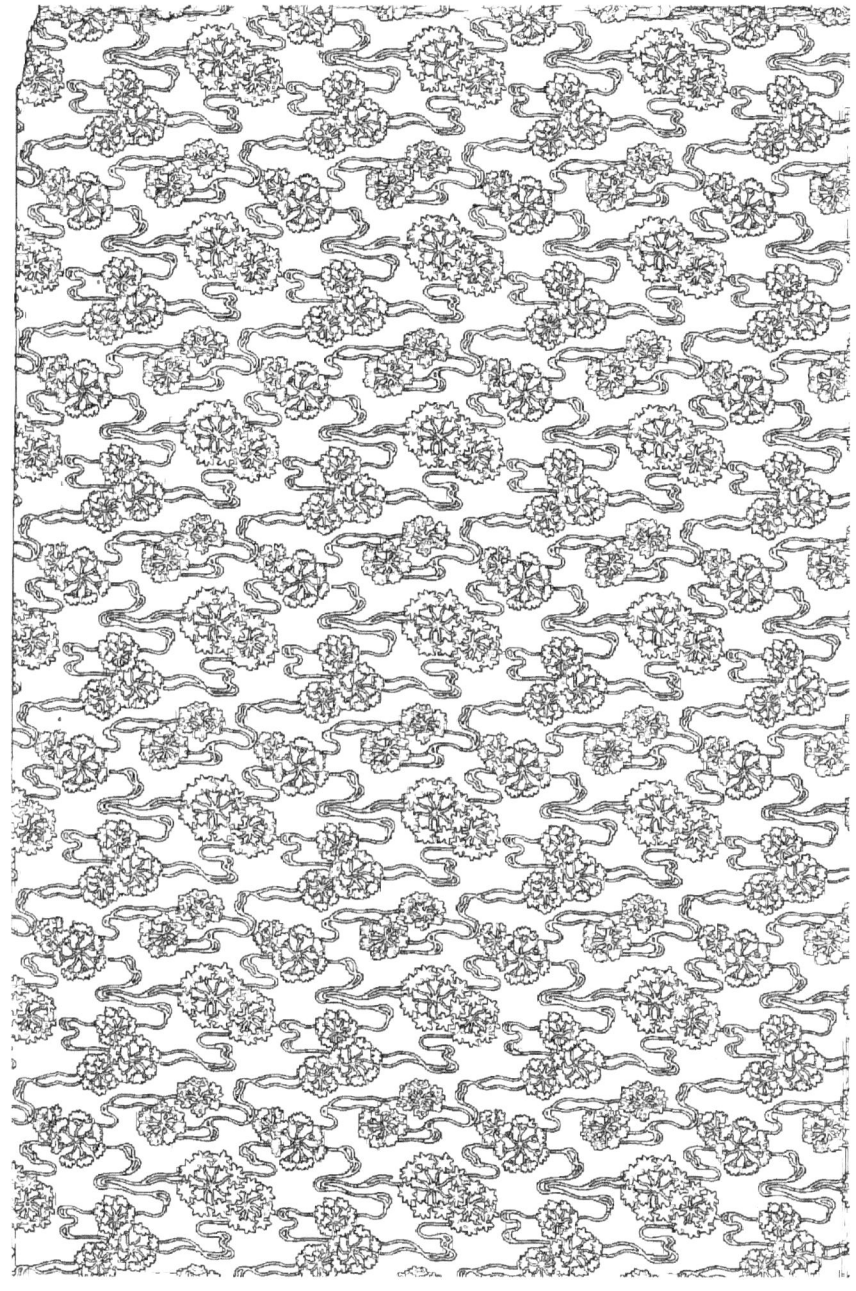

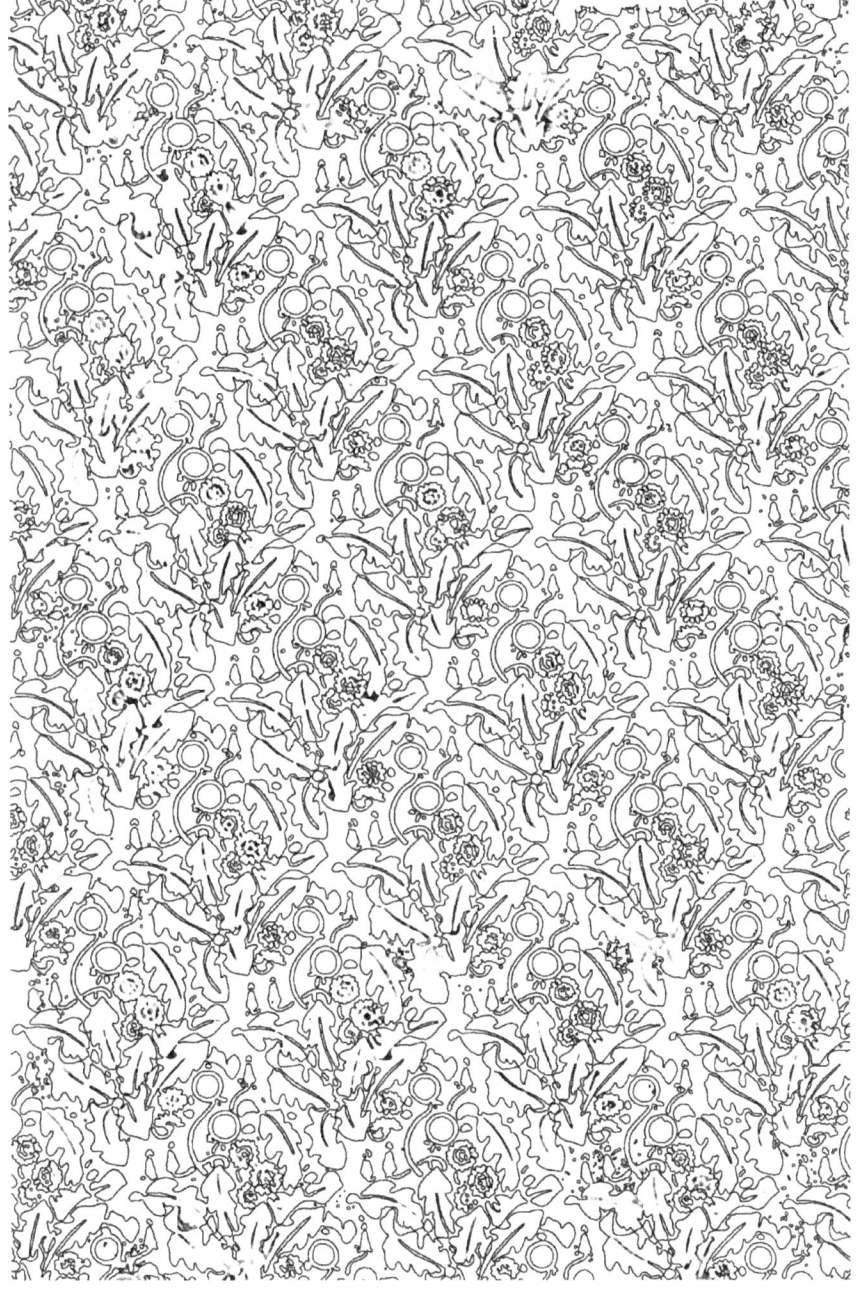

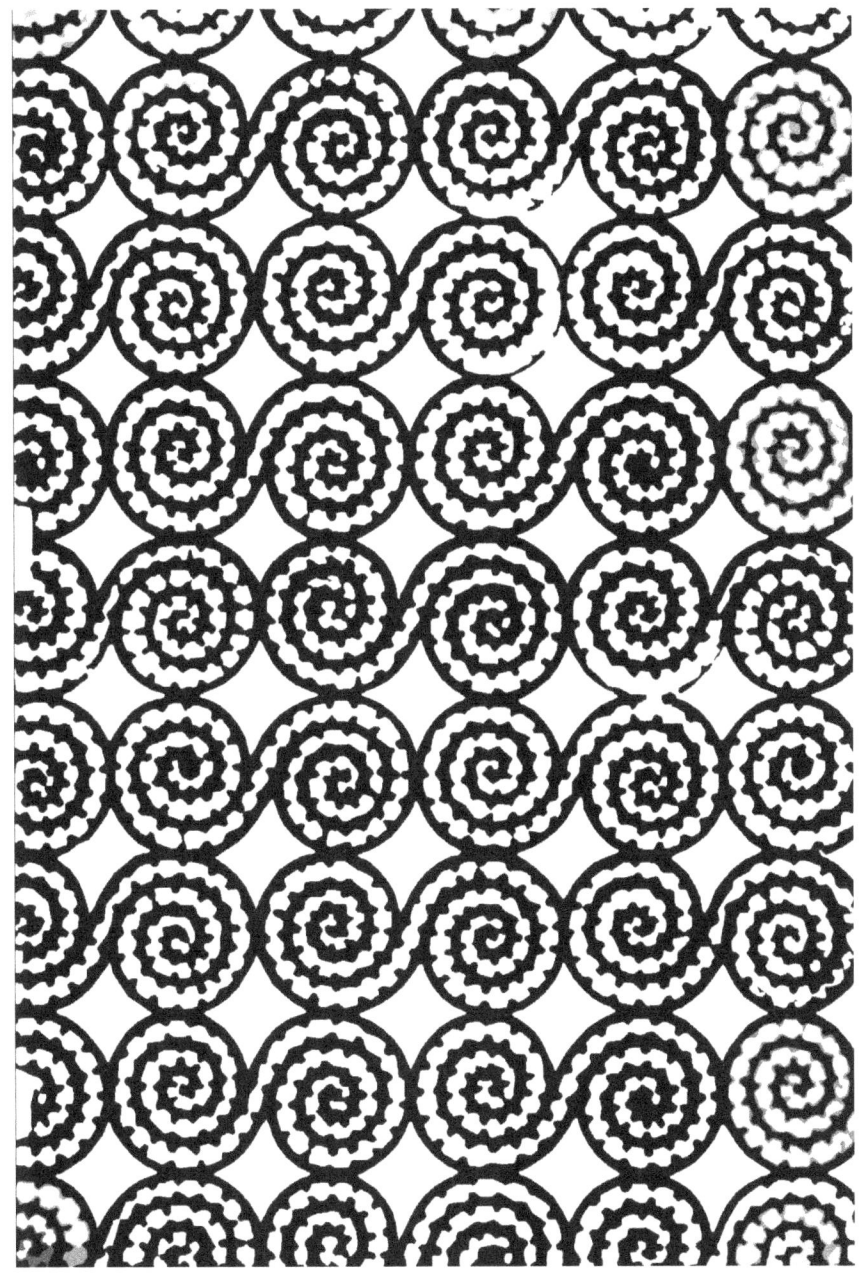

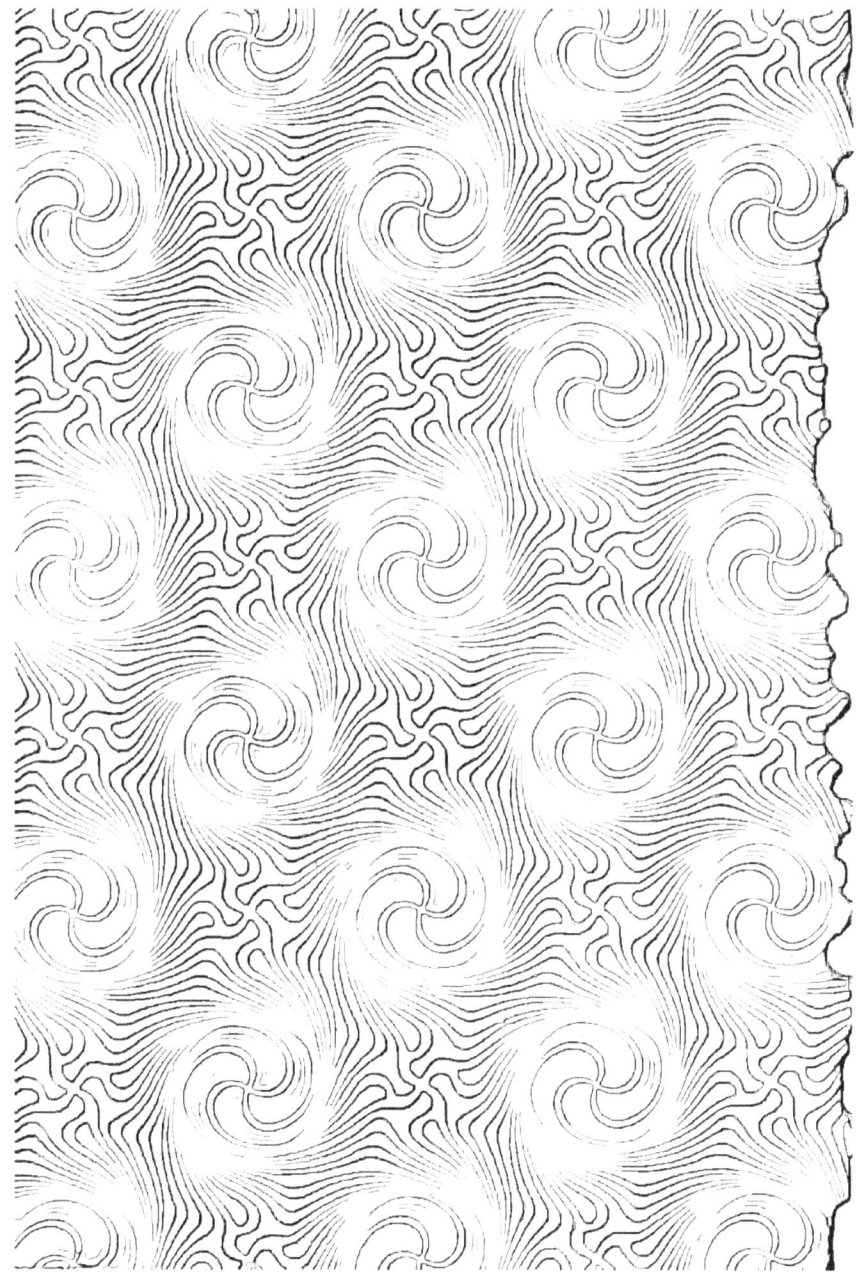

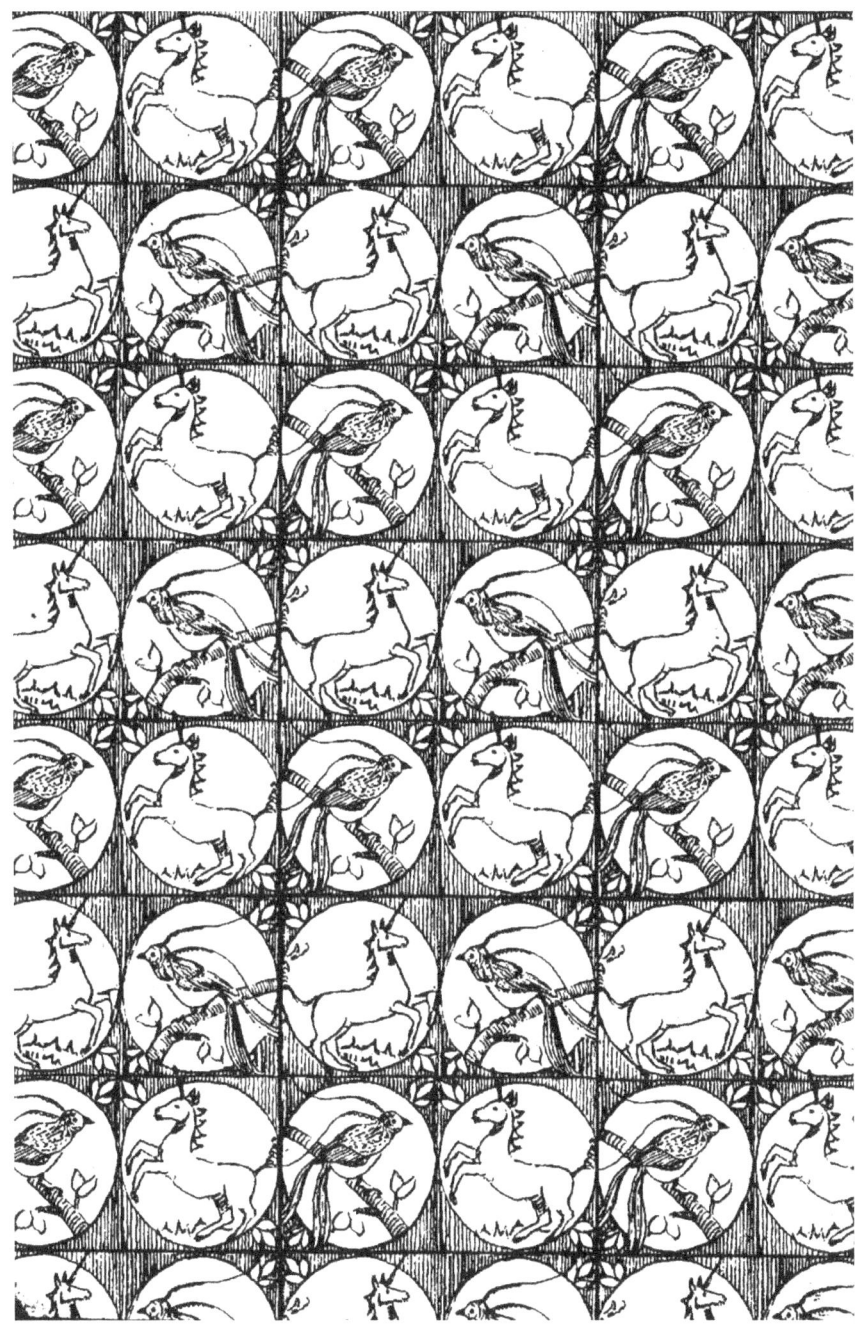

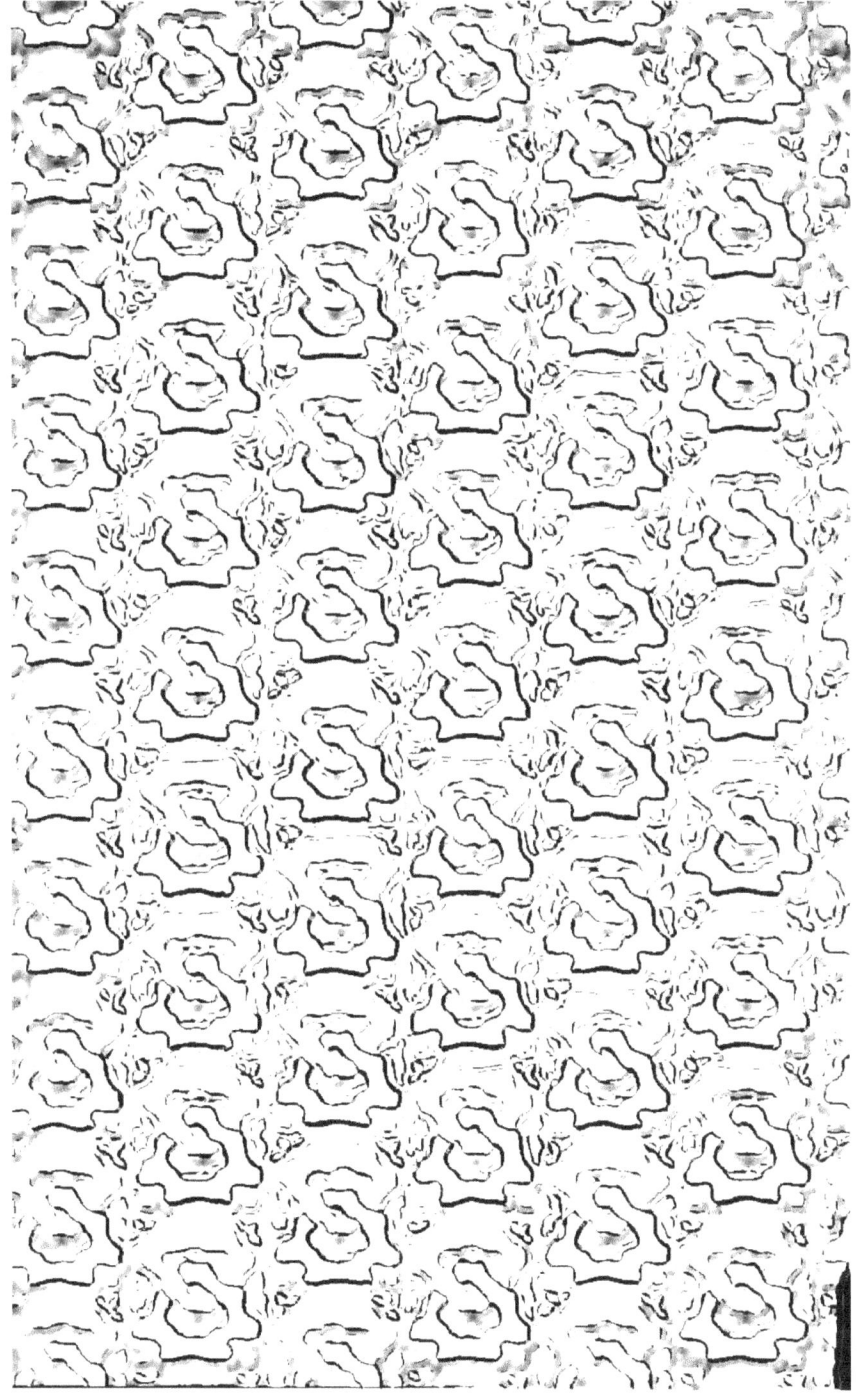

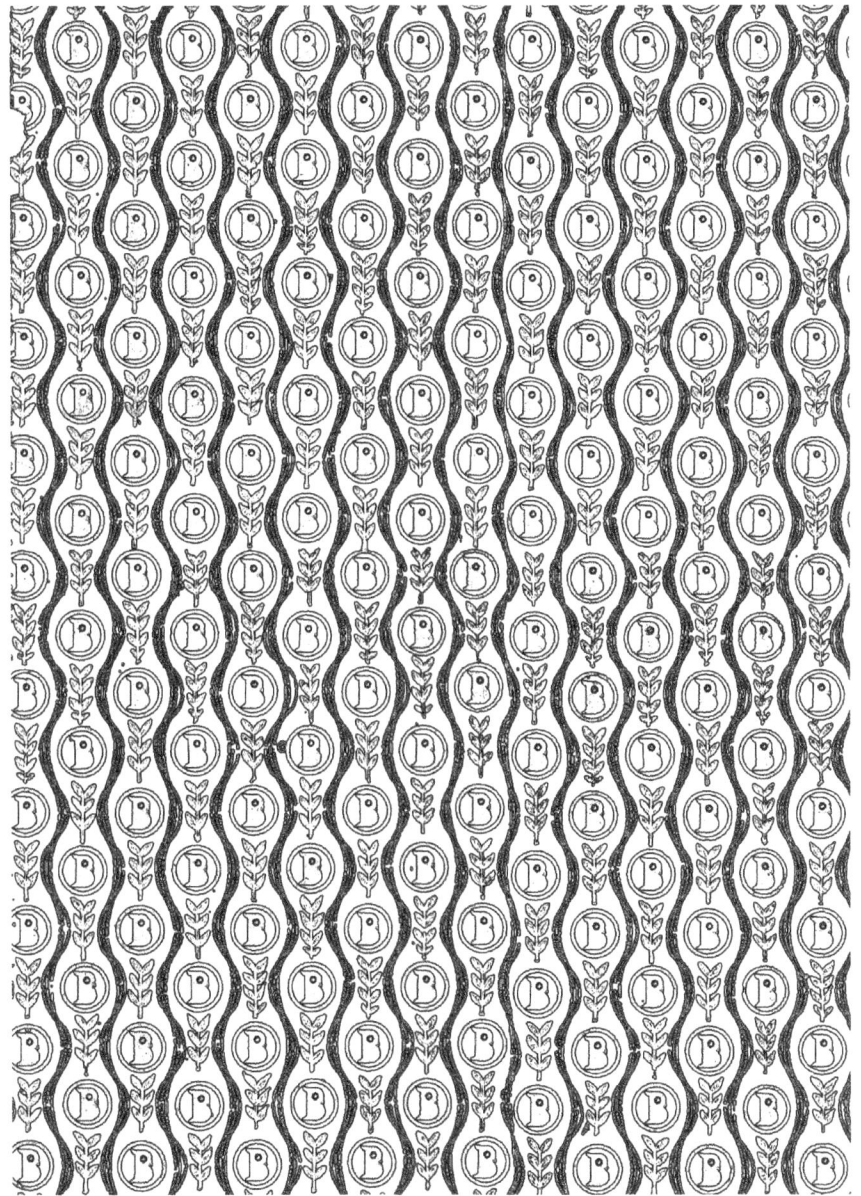

.

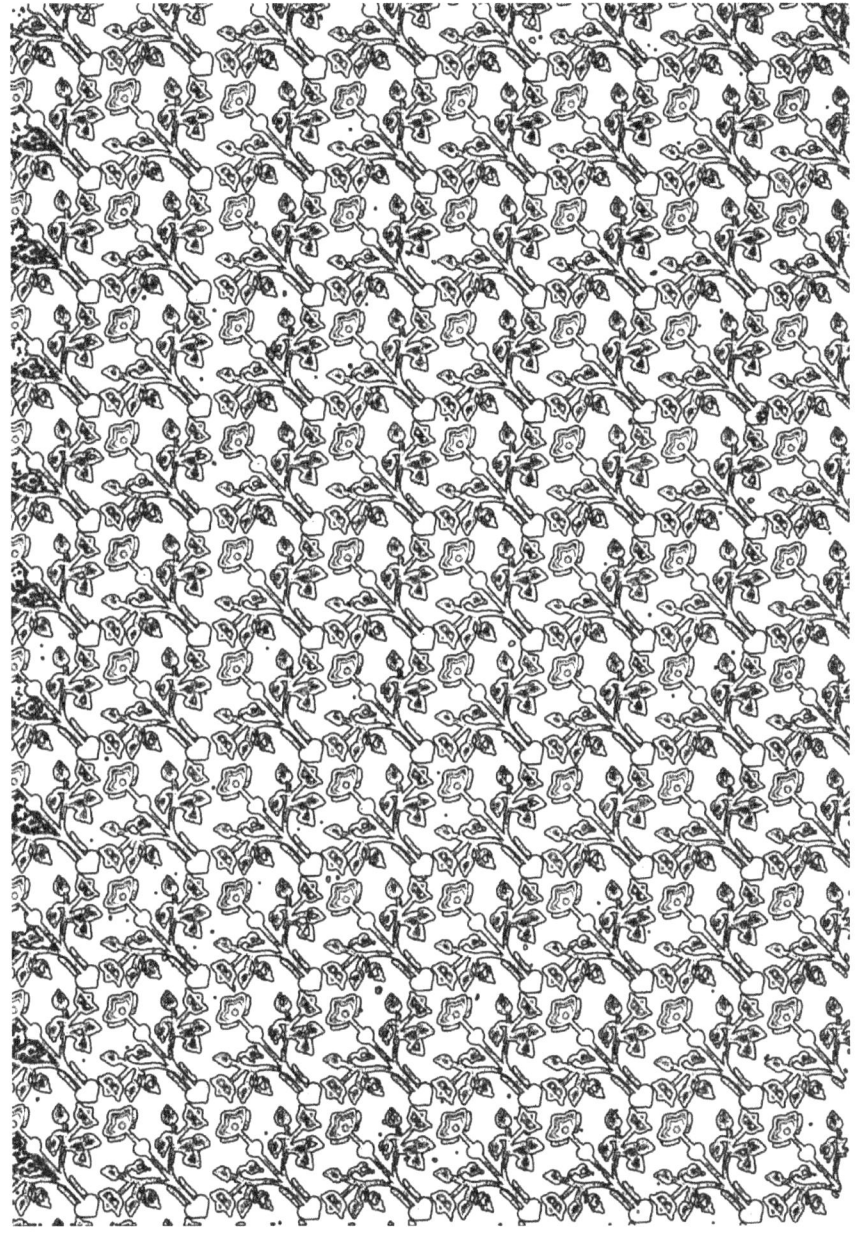

ABOUT THE DESIGNS

These patterns are endpapers designs from books at the Bergen Library in Norway spanning from 1890-1930, converted to facilitate coloring.